Bread Machine Cookbook

Every Day Bread Edition

By

VIOLET CRESS

Contents

1- Basic White Bread

Total Time: 3 hours 25 minutes

Serve: 12

Ingredients:

- 4 ¼ cups bread flour
- 2 tsp sugar
- 2 ½ tsp active dry yeast
- 2 tbsp milk powder
- 2 ½ tbsp butter
- 1 1/3 cups water
- 2 tsp salt

Directions:

Add all ingredients to the bread machine pan according to your bread machine manufacturer's instructions. Set the bread machine to white bread cycle then select medium crust. Press start. Let the bread loaf cool completely. Slice and serve.

Nutritional Value (Amount per Serving):

Calories 192, Fat 2.9 g, Carbohydrates 35.5 g, Sugar 1.5 g, Protein 5.4 g, Cholesterol 7 mg

2-Milk & Honey Bread

Total Time: 2 hours

Serve: 16

Ingredients:

- 3 cups bread flour
- 2 tsp active dry yeast
- 3 tbsp butter, melted
- 3 tbsp honey
- 1 cup milk
- 1 ½ tsp salt

Directions:

Add all ingredients to the bread machine pan according to your bread machine manufacturer's instructions. Set the bread machine to white bread cycle then select medium crust. Press start. Let, the bread loaf cool completely. Slice and serve.

Nutritional Value (Amount per Serving):

Calories 125, Fat 2.7 g, Carbohydrates 22.1 g, Sugar 4 g, Protein 3.1 g, Cholesterol 7 mg

3-Pumpkin Bread

Total Time: 3 hours

Serve: 16

Ingredients:

- 4 cups bread flour
- 2 ¼ tsp active dry yeast
- 2 tbsp sugar
- 2 tbsp vegetable oil
- 1 cup pumpkin puree
- 5 oz milk
- 1 ¼ tsp salt

Directions:

Add all ingredients to the bread machine pan according to your bread machine manufacturer's instructions. Set the bread machine to white bread cycle then select light crust. Press start. Let the bread loaf cool completely. Slice and serve.

Nutritional Value (Amount per Serving):

Calories 146, Fat 2.3 g, Carbohydrates 27.2 g, Sugar 2.5 g, Protein 3.9 g, Cholesterol 1 mg

4-Almond Flour Bread

Total Time: 3 hours

Serve: 12

Ingredients:

- 1 cup almond flour
- 0.25 oz dry yeast
- 1 tsp xanthan gum
- ¼ cup vital wheat gluten
- 2 cup whole wheat flour
- ¼ cup honey
- 4 tsp olive oil
- 1 ½ cups water
- 1 tsp salt

Directions:

Add all ingredients to the bread machine pan according to your bread machine manufacturer's instructions. Set the bread machine to white bread

cycle then select medium crust. Press start. Let the bread loaf cool completely. Slice and serve.

Nutritional Value (Amount per Serving):

Calories 128, Fat 3 g, Carbohydrates 22.9 g, Sugar 5.9 g, Protein 3.4 g, Cholesterol 0 mg

5-Basic Vegan Bread

Total Time: 3 hours 40 minutes

Serve: 20

Ingredients:

- 3 ½ cups all-purpose flour
- 1 ½ tsp bread machine yeast
- ¼ cup ground flax seeds
- 2 tbsp canola oil
- 2 tbsp sugar
- 1/3 cup silk soy
- 1 ½ cups water
- 1 ½ tsp salt

Directions:

Add all ingredients to the bread machine pan according to your bread machine manufacturer's instructions. Set the bread machine to basic bread cycle for 2 lbs loaf then select medium crust. Press start. Let the bread loaf cool completely. Slice and serve.

Nutritional Value (Amount per Serving):

Calories 109, Fat 2.3 g, Carbohydrates 18.7 g, Sugar 1.6 g, Protein 2.6 g, Cholesterol 0 mg

6-Banana Bread

Total Time: 1 hour 40 minutes

Serve: 10

Ingredients:

- 2 eggs, lightly beaten
- 3 medium bananas
- ½ cup pecans, chopped
- 1 tsp baking soda
- 1 ½ tsp baking powder
- 2 cups all-purpose flour
- 1 cup sugar
- ¼ cup sour cream
- 1 tsp vanilla
- ½ cup butter, melted
- 1/3 cup milk
- ½ tsp salt

Directions:

Add all ingredients to the bread machine pan according to your bread machine manufacturer's instructions. Set the bread machine to quick bread cycle then select medium crust. Press start. Let the bread loaf cool completely. Slice and serve.

Nutritional Value (Amount per Serving):

Calories 315, Fat 12.3 g, Carbohydrates 48.4 g, Sugar 3.6 g, Protein 24.9 g, Cholesterol 60 mg

7-Gluten-Free Bread

Total Time: 3 hours

Serve: 16

Ingredients:

- 3 eggs, lightly beaten
- 3 ½ cups gluten-free self-rising flour
- 1 tsp vinegar
- ¼ cup olive oil
- 1 ½ cups almond milk
- 2 ¼ tsp dried yeast
- 1 tbsp xanthan gum
- 2 tbsp sugar
- 1 tsp salt

Directions:

In a bowl, mix flour, yeast, xanthan gum, sugar, and salt. In a separate bowl, mix milk, vinegar, eggs, and oil. Add the milk mixture into the bread machine pan then add flour mixture and mix well. Set the bread machine to basic bread cycle then select medium crust. Press start. Let the bread loaf cool completely. Slice and serve.

Nutritional Value (Amount per Serving):

Calories 113, Fat 9.7 g, Carbohydrates 3.3 g, Sugar 2.3 g, Protein 5.1 g, Cholesterol 41 mg

8-Beer Bread

Total Time: 3 hours

Serve: 16

Ingredients:

- 3 ½ cups flour
- ¼ cup sugar
- 2 ¼ tsp yeast
- 2 tbsp olive oil
- 12 oz beer

Directions:

Add all ingredients to the bread machine pan according to your bread machine manufacturer's instructions. Set the bread machine to basic bread cycle for 2 lbs loaf then select dark crust. Press start. Let the bread loaf cool completely. Slice and serve.

Nutritional Value (Amount per Serving):

Calories 137, Fat 2.1 g, Carbohydrates 25 g, Sugar 3.2 g, Protein 3.1 g, Cholesterol 0 mg

9-Cheese Beer Bread

Total Time: 2 hours

Serve: 10

Ingredients:

- 3 cups bread flour
- 4 oz Monterey jack cheese, shredded
- 4 oz American cheese, shredded
- 10 oz beer
- 1 tbsp butter
- 1 tbsp sugar
- 2 ¼ tsp active dry yeast
- 1 ½ tsp salt

Directions:

Add American cheese and beer in a saucepan and heat until just warm. Stir well. Remove the saucepan from heat and let the mixture cool completely. Add cheese beer mixture into the bread machine pan then add remaining ingredients into the bread machine pan. Set the bread machine to white bread cycle then select medium crust. Press start. Let the bread loaf cool completely. Slice and serve.

Nutritional Value (Amount per Serving):

Calories 246, Fat 7.9 g, Carbohydrates 32.1 g, Sugar 2.2 g, Protein 9.2 g, Cholesterol 22 mg

10-Italian Bread

Total Time: 3 hours

Serve: 8

Ingredients:

- 2 cups bread flour
- 1 tsp active dry yeast
- 1 tbsp olive oil
- 1 tbsp sugar
- ¾ cup water
- 1 tsp salt

Directions:

Add all ingredients to the bread machine pan according to your bread machine manufacturer's instructions. Set the bread machine to basic bread cycle then select medium crust. Press start. Let the bread loaf cool completely. Slice and serve.

Nutritional Value (Amount per Serving):

Calories 136, Fat 2.1 g, Carbohydrates 25.5 g, Sugar 1.6 g, Protein 3.4 g, Cholesterol 0 mg

11-Multigrain Bread

Total Time: 2 hours

Serve: 12

Ingredients:

- 1 ½ cups whole wheat flour
- 1 ½ cups bread flour
- 2 ½ tsp bread machine yeast
- ¼ cup honey
- 1 cup 7-grain hot cereal, uncooked
- 2 tbsp canola oil
- 1 ½ cups water
- 1 ½ tsp salt

Directions:

Add all ingredients to the bread machine pan according to your bread machine manufacturer's instructions. Set the bread machine to whole wheat

bread cycle then select light crust. Press start. Let the bread loaf cool completely. Slice and serve.

Nutritional Value (Amount per Serving):

Calories 173, Fat 2.8 g, Carbohydrates 33.4 g, Sugar 6.3 g, Protein 4.1 g, Cholesterol 0 mg

12-Oatmeal Bread

Total Time: 3 hours

Serve: 10

Ingredients:

- 2 1/3 cups bread flour
- 1 tsp active dry yeast
- ½ cup rolled oats
- ¼ cup honey
- 1 tbsp vegetable oil
- 1 cup water
- 1 tsp salt

Directions:

Add all ingredients to the bread machine pan according to your bread machine manufacturer's instructions. Set the bread machine to basic bread cycle then select light crust. Press start. Let the bread loaf cool completely. Slice and serve.

Nutritional Value (Amount per Serving):

Calories 161, Fat 1.9 g, Carbohydrates 32.2 g, Sugar 7.1 g, Protein 3.7 g, Cholesterol 0 mg

13-Cornbread

Total Time: 2 hours

Serve: 12

Ingredients:

- 2 eggs, lightly beaten
- ¼ cup butter, melted
- 1 tsp vanilla
- ¼ cup sugar
- 4 tsp baking powder
- 1 ¼ cup bread flour
- 1 cup cornmeal
- 1 cup milk
- 1 tsp salt

Directions:

Add all ingredients to the bread machine pan according to your bread machine manufacturer's instructions. Set the bread machine to quick bread

cycle then select light crust. Press start. Let the bread loaf cool completely. Slice and serve.

Nutritional Value (Amount per Serving):

Calories 157, Fat 5.5 g, Carbohydrates 23.8 g, Sugar 5.3 g, Protein 3.8 g, Cholesterol 39 mg

14-English Muffin Bread

Total Time: 2 hours 45 minutes

Serve: 8

Ingredients:

- 3 ½ cups all-purpose flour
- 1 tbsp cornmeal
- 2 ¼ tsp instant yeast
- 1 ½ tsp sugar
- 2 tbsp vegetable oil
- 1 cup lukewarm milk
- ¼ cup water
- 1 tsp vinegar
- 1 ½ tsp salt

Directions:

Add all ingredients to the bread machine pan according to your bread machine manufacturer's instructions. Set the bread machine to basic bread

cycle then select light crust. Press start. Let the bread loaf cool completely. Slice and serve.

Nutritional Value (Amount per Serving):

Calories 169, Fat 3.1 g, Carbohydrates 30.1 g, Sugar 1.5 g, Protein 4.8 g, Cholesterol 2 mg

15-Bran Bread

Total Time: 3 hours 40 minutes

Serve: 10

Ingredients:

- 1 egg, lightly beaten
- 3 cups bread flour
- ½ tsp bread machine yeast
- 5 ½ tbsp wheat bran, unprocessed
- 1 tbsp honey
- 1 tbsp olive oil
- 1 ½ tsp kosher salt

Directions:

Add all ingredients to the bread machine pan according to your bread machine manufacturer's instructions. Set the bread machine to basic bread cycle for 1 lb loaf then select medium crust. Press start. Let the bread loaf cool completely. Slice and serve.

Nutritional Value (Amount per Serving):

Calories 166, Fat 2.3 g, Carbohydrates 31.7 g, Sugar 1.9 g, Protein 4.8 g, Cholesterol 16 mg

16-Rye Bread

Total Time: 4 hours

Serve: 10

Ingredients:

- 2 ¾ cups bread flour
- 1 cup rye flour
- 1 ½ tsp dry yeast
- 1 ½ cups warm water
- 2 tbsp butter
- 2 tsp caraway seeds
- 1/3 cup brown sugar
- 1 ½ tsp salt

Directions:

Add all ingredients to the bread machine pan according to your bread machine manufacturer's instructions. Set the bread machine to basic bread

cycle then select light crust. Press start. Let the bread loaf cool completely. Slice and serve.

Nutritional Value (Amount per Serving):

Calories 208, Fat 3.1 g, Carbohydrates 40.2 g, Sugar 4.9 g, Protein 5.7 g, Cholesterol 40.2 mg

17-Basic Egg Bread

Total Time: 2 hours

Serve: 10

Ingredients:

- 2 eggs
- 3 cups bread flour
- 2 tsp bread machine yeast
- 2 tbsp sugar
- 2 tbsp butter, softened
- 2/3 cup milk
- 1 tsp salt

Directions:

Add all ingredients to the bread machine pan according to your bread machine manufacturer's instructions. Set the bread machine to white bread cycle then select medium crust. Press start. Let the bread loaf cool completely. Slice and serve.

Nutritional Value (Amount per Serving):

Calories 189, Fat 3.9 g, Carbohydrates 32.2 g, Sugar 3.3 g, Protein 5.8 g, Cholesterol 40 mg

18-Peanut Butter Bread

Total Time: 3 hours 40 minutes

Serve: 12

Ingredients:

- 3 cups bread flour
- ½ cup creamy peanut butter
- 2 tsp bread machine yeast
- 3 tbsp brown sugar
- 1 cup +1 tbsp water
- 1 tsp salt

Directions:

Add all ingredients to the bread machine pan according to your bread machine manufacturer's instructions. Set the bread machine to basic bread cycle then select medium crust. Press start. Let the bread loaf cool completely. Slice and serve.

Nutritional Value (Amount per Serving):

Calories 203, Fat 5.8 g, Carbohydrates 31.3 g, Sugar 4.3 g, Protein 6.5 g, Cholesterol 0 mg

19-Buttermilk Bread

Total Time: 2 hours

Serve: 12

Ingredients:

- 1 egg, lightly beaten
- 3 cups bread flour
- 1 ½ tsp bread machine yeast
- 2 tbsp sugar
- 4 tbsp butter
- 1 cup buttermilk
- 1 tsp salt

Directions:

Add buttermilk into the microwave-safe bowl and microwave for 30 seconds or until just warm. Add egg in buttermilk and whisk well. Add all ingredients to the bread machine pan according to your bread machine manufacturer's instructions.

Set the bread machine to quick bread cycle then select light crust. Press start. Let the bread loaf cool completely. Slice and serve.

Nutritional Value (Amount per Serving):

Calories 170, Fat 4.7 g, Carbohydrates 27.1 g, Sugar 3.1 g, Protein 4.6 g, Cholesterol 25 mg

20-French Bread

Total Time: 3 hours

Serve: 12

Ingredients:

- 3 ½ cups bread flour
- 2 tsp active dry yeast
- 1 tbsp canola oil
- 1 ½ tsp sugar
- 9.5 oz warm water
- 1 ¼ tsp salt

Directions:

Add all ingredients to the bread machine pan according to your bread machine manufacturer's instructions. Set the bread machine to white bread cycle then select light crust. Press start. Let the bread loaf cool completely. Slice and serve.

Nutritional Value (Amount per Serving):

Calories 147, Fat 1.6 g, Carbohydrates 28.6 g, Sugar 0.6 g, Protein 4 g, Cholesterol 0 mg

21-Molasses Bread

Total Time: 4 hours

Serve: 12

Ingredients:

- 2 cups bread flour
- 2 ¼ tsp bread machine yeast
- 1 ¾ cups whole wheat flour
- 2 tbsp sugar
- 3 tbsp molasses
- 3 tbsp butter, melted
- 1/3 cup milk
- ¾ cup water
- 1 tsp salt

Directions:

Add all ingredients to the bread machine pan according to your bread machine manufacturer's instructions. Set the bread machine to basic bread

cycle then select light crust. Press start. Let the bread loaf cool completely. Slice and serve.

Nutritional Value (Amount per Serving):

Calories 195, Fat 3.4 g, Carbohydrates 36.2 g, Sugar 5.2 g, Protein 4.6 g, Cholesterol 8 mg

22-Healthy Carrot Bread

Total Time: 3 hours

Serve: 12

Ingredients:

- 4 cups bread flour
- 2 tsp active dry yeast
- 2 tbsp sugar
- 2 tbsp butter
- 1 cup carrot, grated
- 1 cup water
- ½ tbsp salt

Directions:

Add carrot and water into the blender and blend until smooth. Add all ingredients to the bread machine pan according to your bread machine manufacturer's instructions. Set the bread machine to white bread cycle then select medium crust.

Press start. Let the bread loaf cool completely. Slice and serve.

Nutritional Value (Amount per Serving):

Calories 182, Fat 2.4 g, Carbohydrates 35 g, Sugar 2.6 g, Protein 4.7 g, Cholesterol 5 mg

23-Onion Bread

Total Time: 2 hours

Serve: 12

Ingredients:

- 4 cups bread flour
- 3 tbsp dry onion soup mix
- 2 tsp active dry yeast
- 2 tbsp dry milk
- 4 ½ tsp sugar
- 2 tbsp butter
- 1 ½ cups water
- 1 ½ tsp salt

Directions:

Add all ingredients except onion soup mix to the bread machine pan according to your bread machine manufacturer's instructions. Add onion soup mix at the fruit and nut signal. Set the bread machine to basic bread cycle then select light crust. Press start. Let the bread loaf cool completely. Slice and serve.

Nutritional Value (Amount per Serving):

Calories 206, Fat 2.4 g, Carbohydrates 40 g, Sugar 2.2 g, Protein 5.4 g, Cholesterol 5 mg

24-Cinnamon Bread

Total Time: 3 hours 40 minutes

Serve: 12

Ingredients:

- 1 egg
- 3 cups bread flour
- 2 tsp yeast
- 1 ¼ tsp cinnamon
- ½ cup sugar
- ¼ cup butter
- 1 cup milk
- ½ tsp salt

Directions:

Add all ingredients to the bread machine pan according to your bread machine manufacturer's instructions. Set the bread machine to sweet bread

cycle then select medium crust. Press start. Let the bread loaf cool completely. Slice and serve.

Nutritional Value (Amount per Serving):

Calories 197, Fat 5 g, Carbohydrates 33.7 g, Sugar 9.4 g, Protein 4.7 g, Cholesterol 25 mg

25-Quinoa Bread

Total Time: 3 hours

Serve: 12

Ingredients:

- 2 ½ cup flour, unbleached
- ½ cup quinoa flour
- 2 tsp sugar
- 1 ½ tsp active dry yeast
- ¼ cup butter, unsalted
- 1 1/8 cups water
- 1 tsp sea salt

Directions:

Add all ingredients to the bread machine pan according to your bread machine manufacturer's instructions. Set the bread machine to sweet bread cycle then select medium crust. Press start. Let the bread loaf cool completely. Slice and serve.

Nutritional Value (Amount per Serving):

Calories 155, Fat 4.5 g, Carbohydrates 24.6 g, Sugar 0.9 g, Protein 3.6 g, Cholesterol 10 mg

26-Cracked Wheat Bread

Total Time: 3 hours

Serve: 12

Ingredients:

- 6 tbsp bulgur cracked wheat
- 1 tbsp active dry yeast
- 1 ½ cups whole wheat flour
- 1 ½ cup bread flour
- ¼ tsp baking soda
- 3 tbsp butter, softened
- 3 tbsp honey
- ¾ cup warm buttermilk
- 1 ½ cups water
- 1 ½ tsp salt

Directions:

Add water and bulgur in a saucepan and bring to boil for 5 minutes. Drain well and let it cool for 15 minutes. Add all ingredients to the bread machine pan according to your bread machine manufacturer's instructions. Set the bread machine to basic bread cycle then select medium crust. Press start. Let the bread loaf cool completely. Slice and serve.

Nutritional Value (Amount per Serving):

Calories 182, Fat 3.4 g, Carbohydrates 33.1 g, Sugar 5.1 g, Protein 4.8 g, Cholesterol 8 mg

27-Lemon Spice Bread

Total Time: 3 hours

Serve: 16

Ingredients:

- 1 egg
- 2 tsp bread machine yeast
- 3 cups bread flour
- ¼ tsp ground nutmeg
- 1 tbsp lemon, grated
- 2 tbsp poppy seeds
- 3 tbsp sugar
- 3 tsp butter
- 3 tbsp lemon juice
- ½ cup + 2 tbsp water
- ¾ tsp salt

Directions:

Add all ingredients to the bread machine pan according to your bread machine manufacturer's instructions. Set the bread machine to basic bread cycle then select light crust. Press start. Let the bread loaf cool completely. Slice and serve.

Nutritional Value (Amount per Serving):

Calories 118, Fat 1.8 g, Carbohydrates 21.8 g, Sugar 2.9 g, Protein 3.3 g, Cholesterol 12 mg

28-Orange Bread

Total Time: 3 hours

Serve: 12

Ingredients:

- 1 egg, lightly beaten
- 2 ¼ tsp yeast
- 2 tbsp orange zest
- 3 ½ cups flour
- ¼ cup sugar
- 1 tbsp butter, softened
- 1 cup orange juice
- ¼ cup hot water
- 1 tsp salt

Directions:

Add all ingredients to the bread machine pan according to your bread machine manufacturer's instructions. Set the bread machine to white bread

cycle then select medium crust. Press start. Let the bread loaf cool completely. Slice and serve.

Nutritional Value (Amount per Serving):

Calories 175, Fat 1.8 g, Carbohydrates 34.7 g, Sugar 6 g, Protein 4.7 g, Cholesterol 16 mg

29-Cocoa Bread

Total Time: 3 hours

Serve: 8

Ingredients:

- 1 egg, lightly beaten
- 3 cups bread flour
- 2 ½ tsp bread machine yeast
- 1 tbsp vital wheat gluten
- 1/3 cup cocoa powder
- ½ cup brown sugar
- 1 tsp vanilla
- 3 tbsp canola oil
- 1 cup milk
- 1 tsp salt

Directions:

Add all ingredients to the bread machine pan according to your bread machine manufacturer's instructions. Set the bread machine to basic bread cycle then select medium crust. Press start. Let the bread loaf cool completely. Slice and serve.

Nutritional Value (Amount per Serving):

Calories 303, Fat 7.5 g, Carbohydrates 49.5 g, Sugar 10.5 g, Protein 10.6 g, Cholesterol 23 mg

30-Pumpernickel Bread

Total Time: 3 hours

Serve: 10

Ingredients:

- 1 cup rye flour
- 1 ½ cups bread flour
- 2 tsp active dry yeast
- 1 ½ tbsp caraway seeds
- 3 tbsp cocoa powder
- 1 cup whole wheat flour
- 1 ½ tbsp canola oil
- ½ tsp lemon juice
- 1/3 cup molasses
- 1 1/8 cups warm water
- 1 ½ tsp salt

Directions:

Add all ingredients to the bread machine pan according to your bread machine manufacturer's instructions. Set the bread machine to whole wheat bread cycle then select dark crust. Press start. Let the bread loaf cool completely. Slice and serve.

Nutritional Value (Amount per Serving):

Calories 215, Fat 3.2 g, Carbohydrates 42.5 g, Sugar 6.3 g, Protein 5.8 g, Cholesterol 0 mg

31-Anadama Bread

Total Time: 3 hours

Serve: 10

Ingredients:

- 3 ½ cups bread flour
- 2 ½ tsp bread machine yeast
- 1/3 cup cornmeal
- 1 ½ tbsp butter, softened
- 1/3 cup molasses
- 1 1/8 cup water
- 1 tsp salt

Directions:

Add all ingredients to the bread machine pan according to your bread machine manufacturer's instructions. Set the bread machine to basic bread cycle then select light crust. Press start. Let the bread loaf cool completely. Slice and serve.

Nutritional Value (Amount per Serving):

Calories 224, Fat 2.4 g, Carbohydrates 45.1 g, Sugar 6.2 g, Protein 5.3 g, Cholesterol 5 mg

32- Whole Wheat Cinnamon Bread

Total Time: 4 hours

Serve: 10

Ingredients:

- 3 cup whole wheat flour
- ¾ cup raisins
- 2 tsp active dry yeast
- 4 tbsp honey
- ½ cup coconut oil
- 1 cup water
- 2 tsp cinnamon
- ½ tsp salt

Directions:

Add all ingredients to the bread machine pan according to your bread machine manufacturer's instructions. Set the bread machine to whole wheat

bread cycle then select light crust. Press start. Let the bread loaf cool completely. Slice and serve.

Nutritional Value (Amount per Serving):

Calories 292, Fat 11.4 g, Carbohydrates 44.8 g, Sugar 13.58 g, Protein 4.6 g, Cholesterol 0 mg

33-Parmesan Bread

Total Time: 3 hours

Serve: 8

Ingredients:

- 4 cups flour
- 2 ½ tsp yeast
- 1 tsp garlic powder
- 1 tsp Italian seasoning
- ¼ cup parmesan cheese
- 1 ½ cups water
- 1 ½ tsp salt

Directions:

Add all ingredients to the bread machine pan according to your bread machine manufacturer's instructions. Set the bread machine to basic bread cycle then select medium crust. Press start. Let the bread loaf cool completely. Slice and serve.

Nutritional Value (Amount per Serving):

Calories 243, Fat 1.4 g, Carbohydrates 48.6 g, Sugar 0.3 g, Protein 7.9 g, Cholesterol 2 mg

34-Coconut Flour Bread

Total Time: 3 hours

Serve: 8

Ingredients:

- 2 eggs
- 2 ½ tsp yeast
- 1 ½ cups bread flour
- 1 ½ cups coconut flour
- 1/3 cup maple syrup
- 1/3 cup olive oil
- ¼ cup shredded coconut
- ¼ cup oats
- 1 tsp baking powder
- ¾ cup hot water
- 1 tsp salt

Directions:

Add all ingredients to the bread machine pan according to your bread machine manufacturer's instructions. Set the bread machine to quick bread cycle then select light crust. Press start. Let the bread loaf cool completely. Slice and serve.

Nutritional Value (Amount per Serving):

Calories 320, Fat 13.1 g, Carbohydrates 44.7 g, Sugar 8.1 g, Protein 7.7 g, Cholesterol 41 mg

35-Country White Bread

Total Time: 3 hours

Serve: 8

Ingredients:

- 3 cups bread flour
- 2 tsp kosher salt
- 1 ½ tbsp sugar
- 1 ½ cups lukewarm water
- 2 ½ tsp dry active yeast

Directions:

Add all ingredients to the bread machine pan according to your bread machine manufacturer's instructions. Set the bread machine to basic bread cycle then select medium crust. Press start. Let the bread loaf cool completely. Slice and serve.

Nutritional Value (Amount per Serving):

Calories 183, at 0.5 g, Carbohydrates 38.5 g, Sugar 2.4 g, Protein 5.3 g, Cholesterol 0 mg

36-Gluten-Free Rice Flour Bread

Total Time: 3 hours 40 minutes

Serve: 10

Ingredients:

- ¾ cup tapioca flour
- 2 ¾ cups brown rice flour
- 1 tbsp xanthan gum
- 2 ¼ tsp active dry yeast
- 3 tbsp honey
- 3 tbsp olive oil
- 1 ½ cups water
- 1 tsp sea salt

Directions:

Add all ingredients to the bread machine pan according to your bread machine manufacturer's instructions. Set the bread machine to basic bread

cycle then select light crust. Press start. Let the bread loaf cool completely. Slice and serve.

Nutritional Value (Amount per Serving):

Calories 251, Fat 5.5 g, Carbohydrates 55.7 g, Sugar 5.5 g, Protein 4.3 g, Cholesterol 0 mg

37-Semolina Bread

Total Time: 3 hours

Serve: 10

Ingredients:

- 4 cups semolina
- 2 tbsp olive oil
- 2 tbsp sugar
- 1 1/8 cup warm water
- 2 ¼ tsp active dry yeast
- 1 ¼ tsp salt

Directions:

Add water and salt into the bread machine pan. Now add oil, flour, sugar, and yeast. Set the bread machine to whole wheat bread cycle then select medium crust. Press start. Let the bread loaf cool completely. Slice and serve.

Nutritional Value (Amount per Serving):

Calories 276, Fat 3.5 g, Carbohydrates 51.4 g, Sugar 2.4 g, Protein 8.8 g, Cholesterol 0 mg

38-Southern Cornbread

Total Time: 1 hour 30 minutes

Serve: 8

Ingredients:

- 2 eggs, lightly beaten
- ¼ cup butter, melted
- 1 cup milk
- 1 tsp vanilla
- ¼ cup sugar
- 4 tsp baking powder
- 1 ¼ cup flour
- 1 cup cornmeal
- 1 tsp salt

Directions:

Add all ingredients to the bread machine pan according to your bread machine manufacturer's instructions. Set the bread machine to cake cycle and press start. Let the bread loaf cool completely. Slice and serve.

Nutritional Value (Amount per Serving):

Calories 236, Fat 8.2 g, Carbohydrates 35.7 g, Sugar 7.9 g, Protein 5.7 g, Cholesterol 59 mg

39-Brioche

Total Time: 3 hours

Serve: 10

Ingredients:

- 1 egg yolk
- 2 eggs
- 7 tbsp butter, softened
- 1 ¾ tsp active dry yeast
- 2 cups all-purpose flour
- 3 tbsp honey
- 1 tbsp olive oil
- 2 tbsp water
- ¼ cup milk
- ¾ tsp salt

Directions:

Add all ingredients to the bread machine pan according to your bread machine manufacturer's instructions. Set the bread machine to sweet bread cycle then select light crust. Press start. Let the bread loaf cool completely. Slice and serve.

Nutritional Value (Amount per Serving):

Calories 180, Fat 9.3 g, Carbohydrates 20.8 g, Sugar 4.7 g, Protein 3.8 g, Cholesterol 63 mg

40-Whole Wheat Buttermilk Bread

Total Time: 3 hours

Serve: 12

Ingredients:

- 2 cups whole wheat flour
- 2 tsp bread machine yeast
- 1 ½ tsp caraway seeds
- 1 ½ tsp sesame seeds
- ½ tsp mustard seeds
- 1 tsp celery seeds
- 3 tbsp sugar
- 2 cups bread flour
- 2 tbsp olive oil
- 6 tbsp water
- 1 cup buttermilk
- 1 ¾ tsp salt

Directions:

Add all ingredients to the bread machine pan according to your bread machine manufacturer's instructions. Set the bread machine to basic bread cycle then select medium crust. Press start. Let the bread loaf cool completely. Slice and serve.

Nutritional Value (Amount per Serving):

Calories 197, Fat 3.3 g, Carbohydrates 36.4 g, Sugar 4.1 g, Protein 5.4 g, Cholesterol 1 mg

41-Flax Seed Bread

Total Time: 3 hours

Serve: 12

Ingredients:

- 1 1/3 cups whole wheat flour
- 1 ½ cups white flour
- 1 tsp bread machine yeast
- ½ cup flax seeds
- 3 tbsp honey
- 2 tbsp butter, softened
- 1 1/3 cups water
- 1 ½ tsp salt

Directions:

Add all ingredients to the bread machine pan according to your bread machine manufacturer's instructions. Set the bread machine to basic bread

cycle then select medium crust. Press start. Let the bread loaf cool completely. Slice and serve.

Nutritional Value (Amount per Serving):

Calories 166, Fat 3.7 g, Carbohydrates 28.3 g, Sugar 4.5 g, Protein 4.1 g, Cholesterol 5 mg

42-Honey Whole Wheat Bread

Total Time: 2 hours

Serve: 8

Ingredients:

- ½ cup bread flour
- 1 ½ cups whole wheat flour
- 2 tsp yeast
- 1 tbsp sugar
- 2 tbsp honey
- 2 tbsp butter
- ¼ cup water
- ½ cup milk
- ¾ tsp salt

Directions:

Add all ingredients to the bread machine pan according to your bread machine manufacturer's instructions. Set the bread machine to whole wheat

bread cycle then select medium crust. Press start. Let the bread loaf cool completely. Slice and serve.

Nutritional Value (Amount per Serving):

Calories 171, Fat 3.6 g, Carbohydrates 30.8 g, Sugar 6.6 g, Protein 4.2 g, Cholesterol 9 mg

43-Mustard Bread

Total Time: 3 hours

Serve: 12

Ingredients:

- 1 cup whole wheat flour
- 2 cups bread flour
- 2 tsp bread machine yeast
- 1 tsp dill weed
- 1 tbsp brown sugar
- 3 tbsp dry milk powder
- 1 tbsp butter
- 1 tbsp Dijon mustard
- 1 cup water
- 1 tsp salt

Directions:

Add all ingredients to the bread machine pan according to your bread machine manufacturer's instructions. Set the bread machine to basic bread cycle then select medium crust. Press start. Let the bread loaf cool completely. Slice and serve.

Nutritional Value (Amount per Serving):

Calories 136, Fat 1.3 g, Carbohydrates 26.1 g, Sugar 1.8 g, Protein 4.3 g, Cholesterol 3 mg

44-Gluten-Free Sandwich Bread

Total Time: 1 hour 45 minutes

Serve: 8

Ingredients:

- 2 eggs
- 2 ½ cups gluten-free all-purpose flour
- 1 tbsp active dry yeast
- 1 tbsp sugar
- 2 tsp xanthan gum
- 1 tsp apple cider vinegar
- 1 ½ tbsp canola oil
- 1 ½ cups water
- 1 tsp salt

Directions:

Add water, eggs, canola oil, apple cider vinegar, flour, xanthan gum, salt, sugar, and yeast to the bread machine pan. Set the bread machine to basic

bread cycle then select light crust. Press start. Let the bread loaf cool completely. Slice and serve.

Nutritional Value (Amount per Serving):

Calories 181, Fat 4.5 g, Carbohydrates 30.7 g, Sugar 1.6 g, Protein 5.8 g, Cholesterol 41 mg

45-Almond Whole Wheat Bread

Total Time: 3 hours 48 minutes

Serve: 24

Ingredients:

- 2 ¼ cup whole wheat flour
- 2 cups bread flour
- 2 tsp active dry yeast
- ½ cup slivered almonds, toasted
- 4 tbsp honey
- 2 tbsp margarine
- 2/3 cup lukewarm water
- 1 tsp salt

Directions:

Add all ingredients to the bread machine pan according to your bread machine manufacturer's instructions. Set the bread machine to basic bread

cycle then select medium crust. Press start. Let the bread loaf cool completely. Slice and serve.

Nutritional Value (Amount per Serving):

Calories 112, Fat 2.2 g, Carbohydrates 20.3 g, Sugar 3 g, Protein 2.9 g, Cholesterol 0 mg

46-Onion Herb Bread

Total Time: 3 hours

Serve: 16

Ingredients:

- 3 cups bread flour
- 1 ½ tsp active dry yeast
- 2 tbsp sugar
- 2 tbsp dry milk powder
- 1 tsp poppy seeds
- 1 ½ tsp dill weed
- 2 tsp dried onion, minced
- 2 tbsp butter, softened
- 1 cup water
- 1 ¼ tsp salt

Directions:

Add all ingredients to the bread machine pan according to your bread machine manufacturer's instructions. Set the bread machine to basic bread cycle then select medium crust. Press start. Let the bread loaf cool completely. Slice and serve.

Nutritional Value (Amount per Serving):

Calories 110, Fat 1.8 g, Carbohydrates 20.5 g, Sugar 2.1 g, Protein 3 g, Cholesterol 4 mg

47-Pumpkin Pie Spice Bread Loaf

Total Time: 1 hour 40 minutes

Serve: 12

Ingredients:

- 2 eggs
- 1 ½ tsp pumpkin pie spice
- 2 tsp baking powder
- 1 ½ cups all-purpose flour
- 1 tsp vanilla
- 1/3 cup canola oil
- 1 cup pumpkin puree
- ½ cup sugar
- ½ cup brown sugar
- ¼ tsp salt

Directions:

Add all ingredients to the bread machine pan according to your bread machine manufacturer's instructions. Set the bread machine to quick bread cycle then select medium crust. Press start. Let the bread loaf cool completely. Slice and serve.

Nutritional Value (Amount per Serving):

Calories 185, Fat 7 g, Carbohydrates 28.5 g, Sugar 15 g, Protein 2.8 g, Cholesterol 27 mg

48-Irish Soda Bread

Total Time: 2 hours

Serve: 16

Ingredients:

- 2 eggs
- 4 cups all-purpose flour
- 1 cup raisin
- 1 tbsp baking soda
- ½ tbsp caraway seeds
- 1 ½ cups buttermilk
- ½ tsp salt

Directions:

Add buttermilk and eggs to the bread machine pan. Mix together the remaining ingredients and pour over the buttermilk and egg mixture. Set the bread machine to quick bread cycle then press start. Let the bread loaf cool completely. Slice and serve.

Nutritional Value (Amount per Serving):

Calories 159, Fat 1.1 g, Carbohydrates 32.3 g, Sugar 6.6 g, Protein 5 g, Cholesterol 21 mg

49-Amish Bread

Total Time: 3 hours

Serve: 12

Ingredients:

- 2 ¾ cups bread flour
- 1 cup + 2 tbsp warm water
- ¼ cup sugar
- 1 tsp active dry yeast
- ¼ cup canola oil
- ½ tsp salt

Directions:

Add all ingredients to the bread machine pan according to your bread machine manufacturer's instructions. Set the bread machine to white bread cycle 1.5 lbs loaf then press start. Let the bread loaf cool completely. Slice and serve.

Nutritional Value (Amount per Serving):

Calories 161, Fat 4.8 g, Carbohydrates 26.2 g, Sugar 4.3 g, Protein 3.1 g, Cholesterol 0 mg

50-Soft & Light Sandwich Bread

Total Time: 3 hours

Serve: 8

Ingredients:

- 3 ¾ cups flour
- 2 tsp yeast
- 3 tbsp sugar
- 3 tbsp butter
- 1/3 cup lukewarm milk
- 1 cup lukewarm water
- 1 tsp salt

Directions:

Add water, milk, butter, sugar, salt, yeast, and flour into the bread machine pan. Set the bread machine to a basic 2 lbs loaf then press start. Let the bread loaf cool completely. Slice and serve.